Backyard Animals
Earthworms

Anita Yasuda

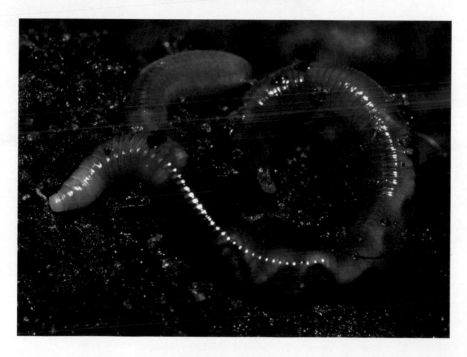

www.av2books.com

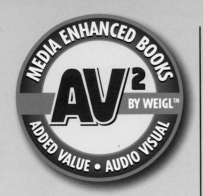

MEDIA ENHANCED BOOKS
AV² BY WEIGL™
ADDED VALUE • AUDIO VISUAL

AV² provides enriched content that supplements and complements this book. Weigl's AV² books strive to create inspired learning and engage young minds in a total learning experience.

Your AV² Media Enhanced books come alive with...

Audio
Listen to sections of the book read aloud.

Key Words
Study vocabulary, and complete a matching word activity.

Go to **www.av2books.com**, and enter this book's unique code.

Video
Watch informative video clips.

Quizzes
Test your knowledge.

BOOK CODE

R 5 4 5 6 2 2

Embedded Weblinks
Gain additional information for research.

Slide Show
View images and captions, and prepare a presentation.

AV² by Weigl brings you media enhanced books that support active learning.

Try This!
Complete activities and hands-on experiments.

... and much, much more!

Published by AV² by Weigl
350 5th Avenue, 59th Floor
New York, NY 10118
Website: www.av2books.com   www.weigl.com

Library of Congress Cataloging-in-Publication Data

Yasuda, Anita.
Earthworms / Anita Yasuda.
    p. cm. -- (Backyard animals)
Includes index.
ISBN 978-1-61690-619-1 (hardcover : alk. paper) -- ISBN 978-1-61690-625-2 (softcover : alk. paper)
1. Earthworms--Juvenile literature. I. Title.

QL391.A6Y37 2011
592'.64--dc22
                            2010045193

Printed in the United States of America in North Mankato, Minnesota
1 2 3 4 5 6 7 8 9 0   15 14 13 12 11

052011
WEP37500

Editor Jordan McGill   Design Terry Paulhus

Every reasonable effort has been made to trace ownership and to obtain permission to reprint copyright material. The publishers would be pleased to have any errors or omissions brought to their attention so that they may be corrected in subsequent printings.

Photo Credits
Weigl acknowledges Getty Images as its primary photo supplier for this title.

Contents

Meet the Earthworm

An earthworm is a small animal that tunnels through **soil**. An earthworm's body is made up of tiny rings covered in hairs. These hairs help the worm move through soil.

Earthworms are **invertebrates**. Instead of bones, an earthworm's body is filled with fluid. Earthworms have external skeletons that protect their insides.

Some earthworms have pinkish bodies, and others are green or brown. Earthworms are toothless and eyeless.

Earthworms eat soil, leaves, and roots. They are important links in many **food chains**. Small birds and animals, including robins, eat earthworms.

Earthworms have a strong sense of touch. They sense vibrations through the fine hairs on their bodies.

Earthworms have five hearts. Similar to a human body, the hearts pump blood through the worm's body.

All about Earthworms

Earthworms are found in North America, Asia, and Europe. Earthworms play an important role keeping soil healthy.

As earthworms tunnel through soil, they make holes in the ground that allow oxygen and water to enter. Tunneling also mixes plant matter from the surface deep into the ground. As the plant matter breaks down, **nutrients** enter the soil. Plant roots can grow deeper and stronger as a result.

There are about 2,700 types of earthworms.

Other Types of Worm

Medusa Worm

Lives deep in the mud volcanoes of the Atlantic Ocean

Acorn Worm

Lives along the ocean floor and in deep oceanic trenches

Giant Blue Worm

Resides in Borneo and the islands of New Guinea

Tubeworms

Found in the Pacific Ocean near the Galapagos Islands

Earthworm History

Fossils show that creatures similar to earthworms have lived on Earth for at least 500 million years. Earthworms have crawled on Earth for more than 120 million years. There are few fossils because earthworms have no bones.

Most **native** North American earthworms are thought to be extinct. They probably died during the last Ice Age, 10,000 to 50,000 years ago. Earthworms only survived in areas untouched by glaciers. Many of the earthworms seen today in North America were brought over by European settlers. These earthworms played an important role in making **fertile** soil for the settlers' crops.

Fascinating Facts

One acre of soil contains one million earthworms. In one year, these worms make roughly 40,000 pounds (18,000 kilograms) of rich soil per acre.

The giant Gippsland earthworm can grow to about 10 feet (3 meters) long. The people who discovered it thought it was a snake.

Earthworm Shelter

Most earthworms live in soil. Some earthworms live on the surface of soil in **organic matter** such as leaves.

The earthworm lives in underground tunnels. These can be more than 5 feet (1.5 m) deep. Earthworms pull organic matter into their **burrow**.

Earthworms like mild and moist weather. They are most active in the spring and fall. When it is cooler, earthworms come to the surface of the soil. When the weather becomes cold, earthworms move deeper into the soil. During winter, some **species** curl into a knot.

Earthworms can live most places where there is enough moisture in the soil. Without enough moisture in the soil, earthworms cannot breathe.

Earthworms live in temperatures ranging from 32 to 89.6 degrees Fahrenheit (0 to 32 degrees Celsius).

Earthworms cannot see, but they can sense light. Sensors on their bodies can tell them if it is light or dark outside their burrow.

Earthworm Features

Earthworms have **adapted** to living in soil. An earthworm's body has two main parts. It has an outer tube that is mainly muscle and an inner tube that digests food. An earthworm has a mouth, which it uses to eat soil as it tunnels underground.

MOUTH
Earthworms have no teeth. They can only eat food that is soft enough to be broken apart or small enough to fit in their mouth. When an earthworm finds something that it can eat, its **pharynx** sucks the food into its mouth.

PROSTOMIUM
The earthworm has a flap of skin that hangs over its mouth. This flap is called the prostomium. It allows the earthworm to sense what is around its mouth. Earthworms use the prostomium to guide themselves through soil.

SKIN

An earthworm's thin skin cannot stand heat or sunlight. Earthworms can easily dry out if placed in sunlight. Living underground helps the earthworm's skin stay moist.

ANNULI

The earthworm is made up of sections called annuli. In order to move, a worm lengthens the front part of its body and pushes through the soil. It then moves its back part up. The muscles along the length of the worm help it to shorten and lengthen.

What Do Earthworms Eat?

Earthworms recycle nature's waste. They eat mainly decaying leaves, animal remains, and other organic material in soil.

With each movement forward, an earthworm takes in more food. Food that enters an earthworm's mouth goes directly into its stomach.

In their stomach, earthworms store tiny pieces of rock. This helps them grind up food that they have eaten.

An earthworm can eat up to one third of its body weight in food each day.

Earthworms can dig tunnels as deep as 15 feet (4.5 m).

Earthworm Life Cycle

Earthworms breed throughout the year. Those living deep in the soil do not have to breed as often. Their young are better protected from **predators** than surface earthworms.

Egg

To produce young, two earthworms make a liquid substance. This substance forms a tube around them. The earthworms lay their eggs inside the tube.

The tube separates from the worms. The ends of the tube seal to form a cocoon.

Cocoon

A **cocoon** is buried in the soil for weeks or months. Each cocoon contains one to 20 eggs.

Soil temperature affects the number of young born. There are fewer young born in the winter.

Juvenile

Only one to five baby worms hatch from each cocoon. Baby earthworms look like tiny white threads. They are not cared for by adults.

Adult

At 12 months of age, earthworms are fully developed. They live between 4 and 10 years. This may be shorter in an area with many predators, such as birds, reptiles, and insects.

Encountering Earthworms

During the day, people often find worms under rocks and fallen logs, or in the deep underground. The worms stay there to escape sunlight. Earthworms come out at night to find food such as leaves and other plant matter. They are sometimes called nightcrawlers because they are often seen at night.

Some people keep earthworms in a bin with organic waste. The worms change people's organic garbage into a substance that can be used in gardens to help plants grow. This is called composting. Composting helps keep the environment clean by reducing the amount of waste that ends up in landfills.

Fascinating Facts

A 22-foot (6.7-meter) earthworm was discovered in South America. It is the largest earthworm ever found.

Charles Darwin studied earthworms for more than 40 years. He felt they were an important part of natural history.

Myths and Legends

Greek philosopher Aristotle said that earthworms were "the intestines of the earth." Many ancient cultures thought the earthworm played a key role in soil health.

Ancient Egyptians valued the earthworm's role in growing crops. The **pharaoh** Cleopatra made earthworms sacred. Egyptians farmers were not allowed to remove earthworms from their land.

Farmers could be sentenced to death if they touched a worm. Cleopatra believed that touching the worm might anger the goddess of fertility. She was thought to be responsible for healthy crops.

In an old form of English, *wyrm* meant snake, dragon, or worm.

Beware the Worm Dragon

This is an English legend about a giant worm.

A long time ago in a small English town, there lived a young boy named John. John loved to fish. One day, John felt a tug on his line. He pulled in his line and discovered a strange-looking fish. It was long and thin like a worm. It was so odd that John decided not to carry it back home. Instead, he threw it down a nearby well. Later, John became a knight and traveled widely.

Back at the well, the strange creature lived. It grew fatter and longer until it outgrew the well. At night, it crawled about the countryside eating cattle, sheep, and even children.

News of this strange worm traveled far. John heard the news and returned home to slay the worm. Afterward the town was safe.

Frequently Asked Questions

Can earthworms move forward and backward?

Answer: Yes, they can move forward and backward. Earthworms usually travel headfirst, because they tunnel by eating as they move forward.

Can earthworms breathe?

Answer: Yes, they breathe through their skin. They coat their skin in a slimy substance that helps pass oxygen into their bodies. If earthworms dry out, they are unable to breathe.

Will a worm live if it is cut in half?

Answer: No, if a worm is cut in half, it will not live. It is a myth that cutting a worm in half creates two worms. If a worm is cut near its end, it can grow new parts.

Words to Know

adapted: changed over time to survive

burrow: a place where an animal lives

cocoon: covering that protects a baby worm

fertile: can produce healthy plants

food chains: a system of organisms dependent on each other for food

fossils: traces of an animal that are left behind in rocks

invertebrates: animals that have no backbone

native: an animal that originates from a given place

nutrients: substances essential to life and growth

organic matter: something that was once alive, such as a plant or a leaf

pharaoh: an ancient Egyptian king or queen

pharynx: a part on a worm that moves in and out of its mouth to get food

predators: animals that hunt other animals for food

soil: the top layer of Earth where plants can grow

species: a group of living things that can breed with one another

Index

23

Log on to www.av2books.com

AV[2] by Weigl brings you media enhanced books that support active learning. Go to www.av2books.com, and enter the special code found on page 2 of this book. You will gain access to enriched and enhanced content that supplements and complements this book. Content includes video, audio, web links, quizzes, a slide show, and activities.

Audio
Listen to sections of the book read aloud.

Video
Watch informative video clips.

Embedded Weblinks
Gain additional information for research.

Try This!
Complete activities and hands-on experiments.

WHAT'S ONLINE?

Try This!	**Embedded Weblinks**	**Video**	**EXTRA FEATURES**
Identify different types of worms.	More information on identification.	Watch a video about earthworm behavior.	**Audio** Listen to sections of the book read aloud.
List important features of the earthworm.	More information on the history of earthworms.	See a worm in its natural environment.	
Compare the similarities and differences between young and adult earthworms.	Complete an interactive activity.		**Key Words** Study vocabulary, and complete a matching word activity.
Test your knowledge of earthworms.	More information on encountering earthworms.		**Slide Show** View images and captions, and prepare a presentation.
	More stories and legends.		**Quizzes** Test your knowledge.

AV[2] was built to bridge the gap between print and digital. We encourage you to tell us what you like and what you want to see in the future.

Sign up to be an AV[2] Ambassador at www.av2books.com/ambassador.